THERE ARE
MONSTERS ABOUT

THERE ARE MONSTERS ABOUT

A fiendish poetry anthology compiled by
Zenka and Ian Woodward

Illustrated by Virginia Salter

BLACKIE

British Library Cataloguing in Publication Data

Monster verse.
1. Children's poetry, English
I. Woodward, Ian   II. Woodward, Zenka
III. Salter, Virginia
821'.008'09282   PR1195.C47

ISBN 0-216-92022-1

Blackie and Son Ltd
7 Leicester Place
London WC2H 7BP

Printed in Great Britain by
Thomson Litho Ltd
East Kilbride, Scotland

ABOUT THE EDITORS

Zenka and Ian Woodward have compiled numerous poetry anthologies for young readers. Their collections include *Witches' Brew* and *Spine Tinglers*. Ian Woodward is also the author of many books, including *The Werewolf Delusion*. The Woodwards have homes in a Hertfordshire hamlet and a Spanish fishing village, where they live with their two children, Philip and Stefanie.

*For Miles
with love*

Schh! THERE ARE MONSTERS ABOUT

We may have progressed in the realms of science and technology but monsters show no signs of dying out. The makers of horror movies and authors of science-fiction novels and comics are constantly creating new monsters to terrify us and chill our blood, and some clever poets are doing their bit, too!

One dictionary defines a monster as 'a large, ugly or frightening imaginary creature; a misshapen animal; an inhumanly wicked person or thing of huge size.' Another dictionary tells us that a monster is 'any legendary, fabulous creature, often partly human, or a compound of two or more animals, such as a dragon.' A third dictionary reveals that a monster can also be 'any huge, extraordinary animal, especially an extinct, prehistoric beast such as the mammoth'.

Whatever the definition, all these monsters, and many more, have been gathered together in this book, their terrible and sometimes gruesome exploits told in verse. Monsters real and monsters unreal, but all certain to grip your imagination. Come with us, if you dare. . .

ZENKA and IAN WOODWARD

THE SWANK

The Swank is quick and full of vice,
He tortures beetles, also mice.
He bites their legs off and he beats them
Into a pulp, and then he eats them.

V C VICKERS

THE MARROG

My desk's at the back of the class
And nobody, nobody knows
I'm a Marrog from Mars
With a body of brass
And seventeen fingers and toes.
Wouldn't they shriek if they knew
I've three eyes at the back of my head
And my hair is bright purple,
My nose is deep blue
And my teeth are half-yellow, half-red?
My five arms are silver and spiked
With knives on them sharper than spears.
I could go back right now, if I liked—
And return in a million light-years.
I could gobble them all
For I'm seven feet tall
And I'm breathing green flames from my ears.
Wouldn't they yell if they knew,
If they guessed that a Marrog was here?
Ha-ha they haven't a clue—
Or wouldn't they tremble with fear!
'Look, look, a Marrog!'
They'd all scream—and *SMACK*
The blackboard would fall and the ceiling would crack
And the teacher would faint, I suppose.
But I grin to myself, sitting right at the back,
And nobody, nobody knows.

R C SCRIVEN

THE HORNY GOLOCH

The Horny Goloch is an awesome beast,
Supple and scaly;
It has two horns, and a hantle of feet,
And a forkie tailie.

UNKNOWN

THE DEMON MANCHANDA

The two-headed two-body,
the Demon Manchanda,
had eyes bigger than his belly.
He walked and talked
right round the world
but every time he opened his mouth
he put his foot in it.

'You're pulling my leg,'
he said to himself.
So he ate his words instead.
I suppose you know the rest:
he went to the window
and threw out his chest.

MICHAEL ROSEN

THE BLACK BEAST

Where is the Black Beast?
Crow, like an owl, swivelled his head.
Where is the Black Beast?
Crow hid in its bed, to ambush it.
Where is the Black Beast?
Crow sat in its chair, telling loud lies against the Black
    Beast.
Where is it?
Crow shouted after midnight, pounding the wall with a
    last.
Where is the Black Beast?
Crow split his enemy's skull to the pineal gland.
Where is the Black Beast?
Crow crucified a frog under a microscope; he peered
    into the brain of a dogfish.
Where is the Black Beast?
Crow killed his brother and turned him inside out to
    stare at his colour.
Where is the Black Beast?
Crow roasted the earth to a clinker; he charged into
    space—
Where is the Black Beast?
The silence of space decamped; space flitted in every
    direction—
Where is the Black Beast?
Crow flailed immensely through the vacuum; he
    screeched after the disappearing stars—
Where is it? Where is the Black Beast?

TED HUGHES

11

THE GOMBEEN

Behind a web of bottles, bales,
Tobacco, sugar, coffin nails,
The Gombeen like a spider sits,
Surfeited; and, for all his wits,
As meagre as the tally-board
On which his usuries are scored.

The mountain people come and go
For wool to weave or seed to sow,
White flour to bake a wedding cake,
Red spirits for a stranger's wake.
No man can call his soul his own
Who has the Devil's spoon on loan.

And so behind his web of bales,
Horse halters, barrels, pucaun sails,
The Gombeen like a spider sits,
Surfeited; and, for all his wits,
And poor as one who never knew
The treasure of the early dew.

JOSEPH CAMPBELL

13

BE A MONSTER

I am a frightful monster,
My face is cabbage green,
And even with my mouth shut
My teeth can still be seen.
My fingernails are like rats' tails
And very far from clean.

I cannot speak a language
But make a wailing sound.
It could be any corner
You find me coming round.
Then, arms outspread and eyeballs red,
I skim across the ground.

The girls scream out and scatter
From this girl-eating bat.
I usually catch a small one
Because her legs are fat;
Or it may be she's tricked by me
Wearing her grandpa's hat.

ROY FULLER

THE HIDEBEHIND

Have you seen the Hidebehind?
I don't think you will, mind you,
because every time you look for him
the Hidebehind's behind you.

MICHAEL ROSEN

HE'S BEHIND YER

'HE'S BEHIND YER!'
chorused the children
but the warning came too late.

The monster leaped forward
and, fastening its teeth into his neck,
tore off the head.

The body fell to the floor.
'MORE' cried the children,

ROGER McGOUGH

MULTIKERTWIGO

I saw the Multikertwigo
Standing on his head,
He was looking at me sideways
And this is what he said:
'Sniddle Iddle Ickle Thwack
Nicki-Nacki-Noo,
Biddle-diddle Dicky-Dack
Tickle-tockle-too!'
None of this made sense to me,
Maybe it does to you.

SPIKE MILLIGAN

JABBERWOCKY

'Beware the Jabberwock, my son!
The jaws that bite, the claws that catch!
Beware the Jubjub bird, and shun
The frumious Bandersnatch!'

He took his vorpal sword in hand:
Long time the manxome foe he sought—
So rested he by the Tumtum tree,
And stood awhile in thought.

And, as in uffish thought he stood,
The Jabberwock, with eyes of flame,
Came whiffling through the tulgey wood,
And burbled as it came!

One, two! One, two! and through and through
The vorpal blade went snicker-snack!
He left it dead, and with its head
He went galumphing back.

'And hast thou slain the Jabberwock?
Come to my arms, my beamish boy!
O frabjous day! Callooh! Callay!'
He chortled in his joy.

LEWIS CARROLL

GRIFFIN

Griffin, Griffin, all alone,
Lying on a sun-warmed stone,
Speak to me of all your lore—
What, O what, are Griffins for?

Are they beautiful or not?
Are they cold or are they hot?
Tell me, Griffin, grave of phiz,
Tell me why a Griffin *is*!

Stretching out your shiny claws,
As if acknowledging applause,
One green eye that greenly winks—
Tell me what a Griffin thinks!

On your stone stretched out at ease,
Free from toil and free from fleas,
You appear like one apart—
Has a Griffin got a heart?

Every Griffin I have known
Lay along a sun-warmed stone
Like a teapot on a shelf,
Being Griffin by itself;

Curling ear and barbed tongue,
Griffin neither old nor young,
Griffin never in a rage,
Griffin wise and Griffin sage;

Ever-Griffin, never-true,
Nothing wounds or touches you;
Griffin murmurs No offence—
Has a Griffin got no sense?

Griffin-brother, kin of mine,
I have learned the countersign.
I will join you on your stone,
Both together, both alone;

Neither young and neither old,
Neither hot and neither cold;
Tell me, Griffin, tell once more—
What, O what, are Griffins for?

R P LISTER

I WISH I WERE A LEVIATHAN

I wish I were a
Leviathan
And had seven hundred knuckles in my spine.
But, oh! I am not,
(Alas! I cannot be)
A Levi-ikey-
A Levi-ikey-mo.
But I'm a firefly
And I'm a lightning-bug,
I can light cheroots and gaspers with my tail.

UNKNOWN

THE HUGE LEVIATHAN

Toward the sea turning my troubled eye,
I saw the fish (if fish I may it cleep)
That makes the sea before his face to fly,
And with his flaggy fins doth seem to sweep
The foamy waves out of the dreadful deep,
The huge Leviathan, dame Nature's wonder,
Making his sport, that many makes to weep:
A sword-fish small him from the rest did sunder,
That, in his throat him pricking softly under,
His wide abyss him forced forth to spew,
That all the sea did roar like heaven's thunder,
And all the waves were stained with filthy hue.
  Hereby I learned have, not to despise,
  Whatever thing seems small in common eyes.

EDMUND SPENSER

LEVIATHAN

Some say Leviathan is just a whale;
    Others believe it is an island mountain—
    Which sometimes disappears; and some are
      certain
That it's a mighty sea-fish, black as coal,

Big as a thousand whales (that's why no sailor
    Shipwrecked upon its shore turns up again).
    But how can such a monstrous brute remain
A mystery, not seen from trawler, whaler

Or jet plane covering the seven seas?
    'What's easier, though,' some clever chap will say,
    'Than for a monster long extinct to stay
Hidden—and full of mischief—in Loch Ness!'

EDWARD LOWBURY

THE MONSTER

A monster who lives in Loch Ness
Is ten thousand years old, more or less:
    He's asleep all the time—
    Which is hardly a crime:
If he weren't, we'd be in a mess!

EDWARD LOWBURY

THE LOON

The Loon, the Loon
Hatched from the Moon

Writhes out of the lake
Like an airborne snake.

He swallows a trout
And then shakes out

A ghastly cry
As if the sky
Were trying to die.

TED HUGHES

THE POBBLE WHO HAS NO TOES

The Pobble who has no toes
   Had once as many as we;
When they said, 'Some day you may lose them all,'
He replied: 'Fish fiddle de-dee!'
And his Aunt Jobiska made him drink
Lavender water tinged with pink,
For she said, 'The world in general knows
There's nothing so good for a Pobble's toes!'

The Pobble who has no toes
   Swam across the Bristol Channel;
But before he set out he wrapped his nose
   In a piece of scarlet flannel.
For his Aunt Jobiska said, 'No harm
Can come to his toes if his nose is warm;
And it's perfectly known that a Pobble's toes
Are safe—provided he minds his nose.'

The Pobble swam fast and well,
   And when boats or ships came near him
He tinkledy-binkledy-winkled a bell,
   So that all the world could hear him.
And all the sailors and admirals cried,
When they saw him nearing the further side:
'He has gone to fish, for his Aunt Jobiska's
Runcible Cat with crimson whiskers!'

But before he touched the shore,
   The shore of the Bristol Channel,
A sea-green porpoise carried away
   His wrapper of scarlet flannel.
And when he came to observe his feet,
Formerly garnished with toes so neat,

His face at once became forlorn
On perceiving that all his toes were gone!

And nobody ever knew
    From that dark day to the present,
Whoso had taken the Pobble's toes,
    In a manner so far from pleasant.
Whether the shrimps or crawfish gray,
Or crafty mermaids stole them away—
Nobody knew; and nobody knows
How the Pobble was robbed of his twice five toes!

The Pobble who has no toes
    Was placed in a friendly bark,
And they rowed him back, and carried him up,
    To his Aunt Jobiska's park.
And she made him a feast at his earnest wish
Of eggs and buttercups fried with fish;
And she said, 'It's a fact the whole world knows,
That Pobbles are happier without their toes.'

        EDWARD LEAR

SEA MONSTERS

Eftsoons they saw an hideous host arrayed
Of huge sea monsters, such as living sense dismayed.

Most ugly shapes and horrible aspects,
    Such as dame Nature self most fears to see,
Or shame that ever should so foul defects
    From her most cunning hand escaped be;
    All dreadful portraits of deformity:
Spring-headed hydras, and sea-shouldering whales,
    Great whirlpools which all fishes make to flee,
Bright scolopendras, armed with silver scales,
Mighty monoceroes with immeasured tails.

The dreadful fish, that hath deserved the name
    Of Death, and like him looks in dreadful hue,
The grisly wasserman, that makes his game
    The flying ships with swiftness to pursue,
    The horrible sea-satyr, that doth show
His fearful face in time of greatest storm,
    Huge ziffius, whom mariners eschew
No less than rocks (as travellers inform)
And greedy rosmarines with visages deform.

EDMUND SPENSER

THE MONSTER

When the sea-monster came to visit us,
Grey harbour-filling bulk with hungry head,
Although our shuddering hundreds ran to stare
In terror on his glaucous length, or pray
Where the sea boiled around him to the shore,
We were not properly prepared for such
An advent: no maidens could be found
Of the right age to satisfy the beast.

Although enthusiastic citizens
Threw fat babies, doddering grandparents,
Nubile beauties into the broth of sea
Around him, the monster snorted once
To show his great displeasure, and withdrew
The enormous serpentinings of his body
Over the horizon, leaving the town to mourn
Its inability to make a sacrifice,
And wonder what it is we want of monsters.

T HARRI JONES

THE KRAKEN

Below the thunders of the upper deep;
Far far beneath in the abysmal sea,
His ancient, dreamless, uninvaded sleep,
The Kraken sleepeth: faintest sunlights flee
About his shadowy sides: above him swell
Huge sponges of millennial growth and height;
And far away into the sickly light,
From many a wondrous grot and secret cell
Unnumbered and enormous polypi
Winnow with giant fins the slumbering green.
There hath he lain for ages and will lie
Battening upon huge seaworms in his sleep,
Until the latter fire shall heat the deep;
Then once by men and angels to be seen,
In roaring he shall rise and on the surface die.

ALFRED, LORD TENNYSON

THE MONSTER

There was an Old Man with a net.
He heard of a Fish in the sea.
He sighed, 'It is strange, I forget
The spot where the monster should be.'
    But even as he yearned,
    His back being turned,
The leisurely Behemoth swam up behind
In a manner by no means ostensibly kind,
    And, not pausing to gloat,
    Neatly swallowed his boat—
Its oars and its rowlocks (the whole of the set),
The Old Man in his sea-boots, Sou'wester, and net;
Leaving nothing at all, to be viewed with regret,
No touching memento at which one might fret—
    No, nothing at all: merely Sea.

WALTER DE LA MARE

NOT ME

The Slithergadee has crawled out of the sea.
He may catch all the others, but he won't catch me.
No you won't catch me, old Slithergadee,
You may catch all the others, but you wo—

SHEL SILVERSTEIN

THE WENDIGO

The Wendigo,
The Wendigo!
Its eyes are ice and indigo!
Its blood is rank and yellowish!
Its voice is hoarse and bellowish!
Its tentacles are slithery,
And scummy,
Slimy,
Leathery!
Its lips are hungry blubbery,
And smacky,
Sucky,
Rubbery!
The Wendigo,
The Wendigo!
I saw it just a friend ago!
Last night it lurked in Canada;
Tonight, on your veranada!
As you are lolling hammockwise,
It contemplates you stomachwise.
You loll,
It contemplates,
It lollops.
The rest is merely gulps and gollops.

OGDEN NASH

THE LAMBTON WORM

One Sunday morning Lambton went
A-fishing in the Wear,
And catched a fish upon his hook
He thowt looked varry queer.
But whatna kind of fish it was
Young Lambton couldn't tell;
He wouldn't fash to carry it hyem
So he hoyed it doon a well.

Now Lambton felt inclined to gan
And fight in foreign wars,
He joined a troop of knights that cared
For neither wounds nor scars.
And off he went to Palestine
Where queer things him befell,
And varry soon forgot aboot
The queer worm doon the well.

Now this worm got fat and growed and growed
And growed an awful size,
Wi' greet big head and greet big mouth
And greet big goggly eyes.
And when, at neets, he crawled aboot
To pick up bits of news,
If he felt dry upon the road
He milked a dozen coos.

This awful worm would often feed
On calves and lambs and sheep,
And swellied little bairns alive
When they lay doon to sleep.
And when he'd eaten all he could
And he had had his fill,
He crawled away and lapped his tail
Ten times round Penshaw hill.

Now news of this most awful worm
And his queer gannins-on
Soon crossed the seas, got to the ears
Of brave and bold Sir John.
So hyem he come and he catched the beast
And cut it in three halves,
And that soon stopped his eating bairns
And sheep and lambs and calves.

NORTHUMBERLAND FOLK SONG

THE MALFEASANCE

It was a dark, dank, dreadful night
And while millions were abed
The Malfeasance bestirred itself
And raised its ugly head.

The leaves dropped quietly in the night,
In the sky Orion shone;
The Malfeasance bestirred itself
Then crawled around till dawn.

Taller than a chimney stack,
More massive than a church,
It slithered to the city
With a purpose and a lurch.

Squelch, squelch, the scaly feet
Flapped along the roads;
Nothing like it had been seen
Since a recent fall of toads.

Bullets bounced off the beast,
Aircraft made it grin;
Its open mouth made an eerie sound
Uglier than sin.

Still it floundered forwards,
Still the city reeled;
There was panic on the pavements,
Even policemen squealed.

Then suddenly someone suggested
(As the beast had done no harm)
It would be kinder to show it kindness,
Better to stop the alarm.

When they offered it refreshment,
The creature stopped in its track;
When they waved a greeting to it
Steam rose from its back.

As the friendliness grew firmer,
The problem was quietly solved:
Terror turned to triumph and
The Malfeasance dissolved.

And where it stood there hung a mist,
And in its wake a shining trail,
And the people found each other
And thereby hangs a tail.

ALAN BOLD

THE WHITE MONSTER

Last night I saw the monster near; the big
White monster that was like a lazy slug,
That hovered in the air, not far away,
As quiet as the black hawk seen by day.
I saw it turn its body round about,
And look my way; I saw its big, fat snout
Turn straight towards my face, till I was one
In coldness with that statue made of stone,
The one-armed sailor seen upon my right—
With no more power than he to offer fight;
The great white monster slug that, even then,
Killed women, children, and defenceless men.
But soon its venom was discharged, and it,
Knowing it had no more the power to spit
Death on the most defenceless English folk,
Let out a large, thick cloud of its own smoke;
And when the smoke had cleared away from there,
I saw no sign of any monster near;
And nothing but the stars to give alarm—
That never did the earth a moment's harm.
Oh, it was strange to see a thing like jelly,
An ugly, boneless thing all back and belly,
Among the peaceful stars—that should have been
A mile deep in the sea, and never seen:
A big, fat, lazy slug that, even then,
Killed women, children, and defenceless men.

W H DAVIES

THE DRAGON OF WANTLEY

This dragon had two furious wings,
One upon each shoulder,
With a sting in his tail as long as a flail,
Which made him bolder and bolder.
He had long claws, and in his jaws
Four and forty teeth of iron,
With a hide as tough as any buff
Which did him round environ.

Have you not heard how the Trojan horse
Held seventy men in his belly?
This dragon wasn't quite so big
But very near I'll tell ye.
Devoured he poor children three
That could not with him grapple,
And at one sup he ate them up
As you would eat an apple.

All sorts of cattle this dragon did eat—
Some say he ate up trees,
And that the forests sure he would
Devour by degrees.
For houses and churches were to him geese and turkeys:
He ate all, and left none behind
But some stones, good sirs, that he couldn't crack—
Which on the hills you'll find.

ENGLISH FOLK SONG

THE DRAGON

On the island of Komodo
   Dragons live for all to see,
Not extinct, there, like the dodo,
   Let alone mere fantasy.

But the tongue of flame that flickers
   From their mouth is just a tongue;
And, though fearsome, they're not fierce—
   Unless you stray too near their young.

EDWARD LOWBURY

A FIERY RED DRAGON

A knight and a lady
   Went riding one day
Far into the forest,
   Away, away.

'Fair knight,' said the lady,
   'I pray, have a care.
This forest is evil—
   Beware, beware!'

A fiery red dragon
   They spied on the grass;
The lady wept sorely,
   Alas! Alas!

The knight slew the dragon;
   The lady was gay.
They rode on together,
   Away, away.

UNKNOWN

AM I QUITE SAFE IN BED?

Are all the dragons dead
And all the witches fled?
Am I quite safe in bed?

HILARY PEPLER

44

THE DRAGON OF STAINES

A dragon who lives down at Staines,
Breathes flame at all low-flying planes;
    He roars: 'You'll catch fire,
    Unless you fly higher,
As witness this pile of remains!'

E O PARROTT

SONG OF THE GREMLINS

When you're seven miles up in the heavens,
   And that's a heck of a lonely spot,
And it's fifty degrees below zero,
   Which isn't exactly hot,
When you're frozen blue like your Spitfire,
   And you've scared a Mosquito pink,
When you're thousands of miles from nowhere,
   And there's nothing below but the drink—
It's then you will see the gremlins,
   Green and gamboge and gold,
Male and female and neuter,
   Gremlins both young and old.

White ones'll wiggle your wing-tips,
   Male ones'll muddle your maps,
Green ones'll guzzle your glycol,
   Females will flutter your flaps,
Pink ones will perch on your perspex,
   And dance pirouettes on your prop.
There's one spherical, middle-aged gremlin
   Who spins on your stick like a top.
They'll freeze up your camera shutters,
   They'll bite through your aileron wires,
They'll cause your whole tail to flutter,
   They'll insert toasting forks in your tyres.

This is the song of the gremlins
   As sung by the P R U.
Pretty ruddy unlikely to many,
   But fact none the less to the few.

ROYAL AIR FORCE SONG, WORLD WAR II;
FROM A VERSION BY A PHOTO-
GRAPHIC RECONNAISSANCE UNIT

THE SPUNKY

The Spunky he went like a sad little flame,
All, all alone.
All out on the zogs and a-down the lane,
All, all alone.
A tinker came by that was full of ale,
And into the mud he went head over tail,
All, all alone.

A crotchety farmer came riding by,
All, all alone.
He cursed him low and he cursed him high,
All, all alone.
The Spunky he up and led him a-stray,
The pony were foundered until it were day,
All, all alone.

There came an old granny—she see the small ghost,
All, all alone.
'Yew poor liddle soul all a-cold, a-lost,
All, all alone.
I'll give 'ee a criss-cross to save 'ee bide;
Be off to the church and make merry inside,
All, all alone.'

The Spunky he laughed, 'Here I'll galley no more!'
All, all alone.
And off he did wiver and in at the door,
All, all alone.
The souls they did sing for to end his pain,
There's no little Spunky a-down the lane,
All, all alone.

UNKNOWN

48

THE GOBLIN

A goblin lives in our house, in our house, in our house,
A goblin lives in our house all the year round.
　　He bumps
　　And he jumps
　　And he thumps
　　And he stumps.
　　He knocks
　　And he rocks
　　And he rattles at the locks.
A goblin lives in our house, in our house, in our house,
A goblin lives in our house all the year round.

ROSE FYLEMAN

STARLIGHT TOM

Who steals round the house by night?
  Nought but Starlight Tom.
Who takes all the sheep by night?
  Nought but he alone.

UNKNOWN

NASTY NIGHT

Whose are the hands you hear
Pulling the roof apart?
What stamps its hoof
Between the bedroom ceiling and the slates?

ROY FULLER

WHAT?

What's in the room I have never entered,
In the heavy gloom, when the velvet is drawn?
What's under the bed, or inside the wardrobe,
  In my own room, when I wake up at dawn?

No one knows what's in there in the cupboard
      When everyone else has gone out,
In the silence that follows that slam of the door,
      After dark, when no one's about;
At the back of the brooms and old shirts and old
  socks,
The Hoover, the shoes, those queer things in a box,
      In the thick smell of polish
In the darkest cobwebby corner, where the roof
  slopes down to the floor.

What's behind the door I have never opened?
  What is at the end of the corridor?
What's round the next bend in the empty lane,
  Further than I have ever been before?

BRIAN LEE

BEWARE, MY CHILD

Beware, my child,
of the snaggle-toothed beast.
He sleeps till noon,
then makes his feast
on chocolate bars
and cakes of yeast
and anyone around—o.

So when you see him,
sneeze three times
and say three loud
and senseless rhymes
and give him all your
saved-up dimes,
or else you'll ne'er be
found—o.

SHEL SILVERSTEIN

53

THE DONG WITH A LUMINOUS NOSE

When awful darkness and silence reign
Over the great Gromboolian plain,
   Through the long, long wintry nights;
When the angry breakers roar
As they beat on the rocky shore;
   When storm-clouds brood on the towering heights
Of the hills of the Chankly Bore—

Then, through the vast and gloomy dark,
There moves what seems a fiery spark,
   A lonely spark with silvery rays
     Piercing the coal-black night,
     A meteor strange and bright:
   Hither and thither the vision strays,
     A single lurid light.

Slowly it wanders—pauses—creeps;
Anon it sparkles, flashes and leaps;
And ever, as onward it gleaming goes,
A light on the Bong-tree stems it throws.
And those who watch at that midnight hour,
From hall or terrace or lofty tower,
Cry, as the wild light passes along:
     'The Dong!—the Dong!
   The wandering Dong through the forest goes!
     The Dong! the Dong!
   The Dong with a luminous nose!'

     Long years ago
   The Dong was happy and gay,
Till he fell in love with a Jumbly Girl
   Who came to those shores one day.

For the Jumblies came in a sieve, they did—
Landing at eve near the Zemmery Fidd,
      Where the oblong oysters grow,
And the rocks are smooth and grey.

And all the woods and the valleys rang
With the chorus they daily and nightly sang—
            'Far and few, far and few,
            Are the lands where the Jumblies live;
            Their heads are green, and their hands are blue,
            And they went to sea in a sieve.'

Happily, happily passed those days!
    While the cheerful Jumblies staid;
  They danced in circlets all night long,
  To the plaintive pipe of the lively Dong,
      In moonlight, shine, or shade.
For day and night he was always there
By the side of the Jumbly Girl so fair,
With her sky-blue hands, and her sea-green hair.
Till the morning came of that hateful day
When the Jumblies sailed in their sieve away,
And the Dong was left on the cruel shore
Gazing—gazing for evermore—
Ever keeping his weary eyes on
That pea-green sail on the far horizon,
Singing the Jumbly chorus still
As he sate all day on the grassy hill—
        'Far and few, far and few,
        Are the lands where the Jumblies live;
        There heads are green, and their hands are blue,
        And they went to sea in a sieve.'

But when the sun was low in the west,
    The Dong arose and said,
  'What little sense I once possessed
  Has quite gone out of my head!'
And since that day he wanders still
By lake and forest, marsh and hill,
Singing—'O somewhere, in valley or plain,
Might I find my Jumbly Girl again!
For ever I'll seek by lake and shore
Till I find my Jumbly Girl once more!'

Playing a pipe with silvery squeaks,
Since then his Jumbly Girl he seeks,
And because by night he could not see,
He gathered the bark of the twangum tree
    On the flowery plain that grows.
    And he wove him a wondrous nose,
A nose as strange as a nose could be!
Of vast proportions and painted red,
And tied with cords to the back of his head:
    In a hollow-rounded space it ended
    With a luminous lamp within suspended,
        All fenced about
        With a bandage stout
        To prevent the wind from blowing it out;—
    And with holes all round to send the light
    In gleaming rays on the dismal night.

And now each night, and all night long,
Over those plains still roams the Dong;
And above the wail of the chimp and snipe
You may hear the squeak of his plaintive pipe
While ever he seeks, but seeks in vain,
To meet with his Jumbly Girl again;
Lonely and wild—all night he goes—
The Dong with a luminous nose!
And all who watch at the midnight hour,
From hall or terrace or lofty tower,
Cry, as they trace the meteor bright,
Moving along through the dreary night—
'This is the hour when forth he goes,
The Dong with a luminous nose!
Yonder—over the plain he goes;
　　He goes!
　　He goes;
The Dong with a luminous nose!'

EDWARD LEAR

I AM JOJO

I am Jojo—
give me the sun to eat.
I am Jojo—
give me the moon to suck.

The waters of my mouth
will put out the fires of the sun;
the waters of my mouth
will melt the light of the moon.

Day becomes night,
night becomes day.
I am Jojo—
Listen to what I say.

MICHAEL ROSEN

THE SATYR'S CATCH

Buzz, quoth the blue fly,
  Hum, quoth the bee:
Buzz and hum, they cry,
  And so do we.
In his ear, in his nose,
  Thus, do you see?
He ate the dormouse,
  Else it was he.

BEN JONSON

THE ROARING DEVIL

St Dunstan, as the story goes,
Once pulled the devil by the nose
With red hot tongs, which made him roar,
That could be heard ten miles or more.

UNKNOWN

ODE TO AN EXTINCT DINOSAUR

Iguanadon, I loved you,
With all your spiky scales,
Your massive jaws,
Impressive claws,
And teeth like horseshoe nails.

Iguanadon, I loved you.
It moved me close to tears
When first I read
That you've been dead
For ninety million years.

DOUG MacLEOD

HOW THE DINOSAUR GOT HERE

(My daughter Jane, at the age of ten, said, 'The dinosaurs came from the moon.' When asked how they got to the earth, she said, 'They fell.'— S M)

'Daddy, what's a dinosaur?'
Said my daughter Jane.
'The dinosaur was a giant beast
That will never be seen again.'

'Where did they all come from?'
'Now that I cannot say.'
And at this information,
She turned and walked away.

She must have thought about it,
For later that afternoon
She said to me, 'I know! I know!
They all came from the moon!'

'If that is true, my daughter,
Would you, pray, please tell
Exactly how they got here.'
She said, 'Of course—they fell!'

SPIKE MILLIGAN

PLESIOSAURUS

There once was a Plesiosaurus,
Who lived when the earth was all porous;
    But it fainted with shame
    When it first heard its name,
And departed long ages before us.

UNKNOWN

THE ICHTHYOSAURUS

This poor beast found a doleful end—
It makes me weep to tell it:
One day it overheard its name,
And then it pined and died of shame
Because it could not spell it.

JOHN JOY BELL

THE MAMMOTH

The mammoth is strong,
The mammoth is brave.
But dear, oh dear,
He could do with a shave.

TOM STANIER

DIPLODOCUS

Behold the mighty dinosaur,
Famous in prehistoric lore,
Not only for his power and strength
But for his intellectual length.
You will observe from these remains
The creature had two sets of brains—
One in his head (the usual place),
The other at his spinal base.
No problem bothered him a bit;
He made just head and tail of it.
So wise was he, so wise and solemn,
Each thought filled just a spinal column.
If one brain found the pressure strong,
It passed a few ideas along.
If something slipped his forward mind,
'Twas rescued by the one behind.
And if in error he was caught
He had a saving afterthought.
As he thought twice before he spoke
He had no judgement to revoke.
Thus he could think without congestion
Upon both sides of every question.
Oh, gaze upon this model beast,
Defunct ten million years at least.

BERT L TAYLOR

PTERODACTYL

There was once a Jill who loved her Jack till
She fell head over heels for a Pterodactyl.
This went on as a matter of fact till
She found out he was too utterly prehistoric for words.

ALISTAIR SAMPSON

68

SABRETOOTH

Sabretooth, oh Sabretooth,
You really are spectacular.
Sabretooth, oh Sabretooth,
You're very like Count Dracula.

TOM STANIER

RHAMPHORYNCHUS
(The flying reptile)

Look, as he swoops from the cliff's rugged face,
   His squadrons of teeth instant death
To careless fish basking in shallow seas
   And lizards short of breath.

His tough skin is cracked and worn as old boots;
   His cries blood-curdle the night.
A Dracula beast with claws on his wings
   He glides ... the world's first kite.

WES MAGEE

VAMPIRES

The vampires that bite necks in gangs,
Like a blood that is tasty and tangs;
    When they've guzzled enough
    Of the hot, pulsing stuff,
They say to their teeth: 'Thank you, fangs!'

TIM HOPKINS

SOFTLY THE VAMPIRE

Softly the Vampire
  Sang to the Snail,
'You caught the Nightmare,
  I held her tail.
But while the Beetle
  Crowed on the Post,
Deep in the Greybeard
  I drowned the Ghost.'

Greenly the Wildfire
  Opened his eyes,
Sang to the Corpse-light,
  'Come, bake the pies!
Heed not the Ghoul, love!
  Trust not his smile,
Out of the Mosque, love,
  He stole the tile.'

CHARLES GODREY LELAND

THE VAMPIRE

The night is still and sombre,
and in the murky gloom,
arisen from his slumber,
the vampire leaves his tomb.

His eyes are pools of fire,
his skin is icy white,
and blood his one desire
this woebegotten night.

Then through the silent city
he makes his silent way,
prepared to take no pity
upon his hapless prey.

An open window beckons,
he grins a hungry grin,
and, pausing not one second,
he swiftly climbs within.

And there, beneath her covers,
his victim lies in sleep.
With fangs agleam, he hovers
and with those fangs, bites deep.

The vampire drinks till sated,
he fills his every pore,
and then, his thirst abated,
licks clean the dripping gore.

With powers now replenished,
his thirst no longer burns.
His quest this night is finished,
so to his tomb he turns,

and there awhile in silence
he'll rest beneath the mud
until, with thoughts of violence,
he wakes and utters ... blood!

JACK PRELUTSKY

TWINKLE, TWINKLE, LITTLE BAT!

Twinkle, twinkle, little bat!
How I wonder what you're at!
Up above the world you fly,
Like a tea-tray in the sky.

LEWIS CARROLL

THE BAT

By day the bat is cousin to the mouse.
He likes the attic of an ageing house.

His fingers make a hat about his head.
His pulse beat is so slow we think him dead.

He loops in crazy figures half the night
Among the trees that face the corner light.

But when he brushes up against a screen,
We are afraid of what our eyes have seen.

For something is amiss or out of place
When mice with wings can wear a human face.

THEODORE ROETHKE

THE WOLFMAN

Even a man who is pure in heart,
And says his prayers by night,
May become a wolf when the wolfsbane blooms
And the autumn moon is bright.

CURT SIODMAK

THE WEREWOLF

The full moon glows, foreboding,
and I quake from head to feet,
for this night I know, in the town below,
the werewolf prowls the street.

He stalks with stealth and cunning
in his search for a soul to eat.
With matted hair and jaws that tear,
the werewolf prowls the street.

His face is filled with fury
as his brain cries out for meat,
and on his prey shall not see day
for the werewolf prowls the street.

So I shake beneath my covers
and I shiver in my sheet,
and I cower in my bed with a pillow on my head,
as the werewolf prowls the street.

JACK PRELUTSKY

THE GHOUL

The gruesome ghoul, the grisly ghoul,
without the slightest noise
waits patiently beside the school
to feast on girls and boys.

He lunges fiercely through the air
as they come out to play,
then grabs a couple by the hair
and drags them far away.

He cracks their bones and snaps their backs
and squeezes out their lungs;
he chews their thumbs like candy snacks
and pulls apart their tongues.

He slices their stomachs and bites their hearts
and tears their flesh to shreds;
he swallows their toes like toasted tarts
and gobbles down their heads.

Fingers, elbows, hands and knees
and arms and legs and feet—
he eats them with delight and ease,
for every part's a treat.

And when the gruesome, grisly ghoul
has nothing left to chew,
he hurries to another school
and waits ... perhaps for you.

JACK PRELUTSKY

GIANT

A giant
  is someone
    ten miles high,
      whose feet
        touch the ground
          and whose head
          hits the sky.

And if I
  saw a giant
    walking down
      our way,
        I wouldn't stop
          but I'd run away
            and hide in a doorway
            quiet as a fly ...

              And I wouldn't come out till
              he'd gone by!

IVY O EASTWICK

IN THE ORCHARD

There was a giant by the orchard wall,
Peeping about on this side and on that,
And feeling in the trees. He was as tall
As the big apple tree, and twice as fat:
His beard poked out, all bristly-black, and there
Were leaves and gorse and heather in his hair.

He held a blackthorn club in his right hand,
And plunged the other into every tree,
Searching for something—you could stand
Beside him and not reach up to his knee,
So big he was—I trembled lest he should
Come trampling, round-eyed, down to where I stood.

I tried to get away—but, as I slid
Under a bush, he saw me, and he bent
Down deep at me, and said, *'Where is she hid?'*
I pointed over there, and off he went—
But, while he searched, I turned and simply flew
Round by the lilac bushes back to you.

JAMES STEPHENS

THE SLEEPY GIANT

My age is three hundred and seventy-two,
    And I think, with the deepest regret,
How I used to pick up and voraciously chew
    The dear little boys whom I met.

I've eaten them raw, in their holiday suits;
    I've eaten them curried with rice;
I've eaten them baked, in their jackets and boots,
    And found them exceedingly nice.

But now that my jaws are weak for such fare,
    I think it exceedingly rude
To do such a thing, when I'm quite well aware
    Little boys do not like to be chewed.

And so I contentedly live upon eels,
    And try to do nothing amiss,
And I pass all the time I can spare from my meals
    In innocent slumber—like this.

CHARLES EDWARD CARRYL

GIANT THUNDER

Giant Thunder, striding home,
Wonders if his supper's done.

'Hag wife, hag wife, bring me my bones!'
'They are not done,' the old hag moans.

'Not done? Not done?' the giant roars
And heaves his old wife out of doors.

Cries he, 'I'll have them, cooked or not!'
But overturns the cooking-pot.

He flings the burning coals about;
See how the lightning flashes out!

Upon the gale the old hag rides,
The cloudy moon for terror hides.

All the world with thunder quakes;
Forest shudders, mountain shakes;
From the cloud the rainstorm breaks;
Village ponds are turned to lakes;
Every living creature wakes.

Hungry giant, lie you still!
Stamp no more from hill to hill—
Tomorrow you shall have your fill.

JAMES REEVES

THE GIANT

Fee, fie, fo, fum!
I smell the blood of an Englishman.
Be he alive, or be he dead,
I'll grind his bones to make my bread.

UNKNOWN

THE GOOPS

The Goops they lick their fingers,
And the Goops they lick their knives;
They spill their broth on the tablecloth—
Oh they lead disgusting lives!
The Goops they talk while eating,
And loud and fast they chew;
And that is why I'm glad that I
Am not a Goop—are you?

GELETT BURGESS

MORE ABOUT BLUNDERBORE

It seems the giant Blunderbore
Is taller than a human door.
In fact, suppose him waiting to come in
All that you'd see would be a boot and shin.

But usually it's someone else
When we get up to answer bells.
And even were it actually giant B
He'd not push in much farther than his knee.

The following are the times or places
To guard against his hideous faces
(Or, more particularly, his appetite,
Which takes in children at a casual bite):

When climbing any garden tree
That's shot up rather suddenly;
Seeing a figure with a second head;
Or switching off the light to go to bed.

ROY FULLER

THE TRUTH ABOUT THE ABOMINABLE FOOTPRINT

The Yeti's a beast,
Who lives in the East
  And suffers a lot from BO.
His hot hairy feet
Stink out the street,
  So he cools them off in the snow.

MICHAEL BALDWIN

A GOOD NIGHT

From witches and wizards and long-tailed buzzards,
And creeping things that run in hedge bottoms,
Good Lord deliver us.

UNKNOWN

INDEX OF FIRST LINES

ACKNOWLEDGEMENTS

The authors and Publishers would like to thank the following for their kind permission to reproduce copyright material in this book:

Jonathan Cape and the Executors of the W H Davies Estate for 'The White Monster' by W H Davies from *The Complete Poems of W H Davies*; The Literary Trustees of Walter de la Mare and The Society of Authors as their representative for 'The Monster' by Walter de la Mare; André Deutsch for 'Be a Monster', 'Nasty Night' and 'More About Blunderbore' from *Poor Roy* by Roy Fuller; The Society of Authors as the literary representative of the Estate of Rose Fyleman for 'The Goblin' by Rose Fyleman; The Gomer Press for 'The Monster' by T Harri Jones from *The Beaver Book of Creepy Verse*; Tim Hopkins for 'Vampires' by Tim Hopkins; Faber and Faber for 'The Black Beast' from *Crow* and 'The Loon' from *Under the North Star*, both by Ted Hughes; Penguin Books for 'What?' from *Late Home* by Brian Lee, published by Kestrel Books, 1976, © 1976 Brian Lee; André Deutsch for 'Griffin' by R P Lister from *The Idle Demon*; Edward Lowbury for 'Leviathan', 'The Monster' and 'The Dragon' from *Green Magic* by Edward Lowbury; A D Peters and Co Ltd for 'He's Behind Yer!' by Roger McGough from *Strictly Private*, published by Kestrel Books; Penguin Books Australia for 'Ode to An Extinct Dinosaur' by Doug MacLeod from *In the Garden of Badthings*; Wes Magee for 'Rhamphorhyncus' by Wes Magee from *A Fourth Poetry Book*, compiled by John Foster and published by Oxford University Press; Michael Joseph in association with M & J Hobbs for 'Multikertwigo' and 'How the Dinosaur Got Here' by Spike Milligan from *Unspun Socks from a Chicken's Laundry*; Curtis Brown and Little, Brown and Co for 'The Wendigo' by Ogden Nash from *Verses from 1929 On* © 1953 by Ogden Nash; E O Parrott for 'The Dragon of Staines' by E O Parrott from *Limerick Delight*; Greenwillow Books (A Division of William Morrow and Co) and A & C Black Ltd for 'The Vampire', 'The Werewolf' and 'The Ghoul' from *Nightmares: Poems to Trouble Your Sleep* by Jack Prelutsky © 1976 by Jack Prelutsky; The James Reeves Estate for 'Giant Thunder' from *More Prefabulous Animiles* by James Reeves © The James Reeves Estate; Faber and Faber and Doubleday Inc, New York, for 'The Bat' by Theodore